TAROT ARCHETYPES

The Court Cards Unmasked

ANDREW LAYCOCK

Copyright © Andrew Laycock 2025.

All Rights Reserved

Any reproduction of part or all of the contents in any form, with the exception of brief quotations, is prohibited without the express written permission of the copyright owner.

Table of Contents

Introduction 1
The Court of Cups 5
    The Page of Cups 5
    The Knight of Cups 9
    The Queen of Cups 13
    The King of Cups 17
The Court of Pentacles 21
    The Page of Pentacles 21
    The Knight of Pentacles 25
    The Queen of Pentacles 29
    The King of Pentacles 33
The Court of Swords 37
    The Page of Swords 37
    The Knight of Swords 41
    The Queen of Swords 45
    The King of Swords 49
The Court of Wands 53
    The Page of Wands 53
    The Knight of Wands 57
    The Queen of Wands 61
    The King of Wands 65
Who am I? 68
Quizzes 69
About the Author 76

Introduction

The court cards of the tarot are often considered the most challenging part of the tarot deck to interpret. Unlike the numbered cards, they do not always guide us through a situation or event, but instead represent people, personalities, attitudes, and approaches to life. They are the living, breathing personalities of the tarot, from the wide-eyed curiosity of the Page to the hard-won wisdom of the King. Through the sixteen cards of the tarot court, we can understand how we, and others, act, respond, and learn to whatever life may throw at us.

This book offers a practical and structured way to understand the court cards by focusing on their characters. Through these pages we are shown the court cards as distinct personalities that move through life with strengths, weaknesses, challenges, and lessons to learn. Within the tarot court there is the Enthusiastic Campaigner who burns with innovative ideas, the Discerning Judge whose clarity cuts through confusion, the Devoted Steward who nurtures all they touch, and the Wise Architect who builds lasting legacies. They, and the other dozen characters each give us another way to connect the tarot to real-world situations and the behaviours we demonstrate when faced with them.

The Pages are young and exploratory, focused on learning and discovery. The Knights act, often with passion and urgency. The Queens represent internal, deep-rooted knowledge and emotional intelligence. The Kings demonstrate leadership, responsibility, and long-term vision. These four distinct characters reflect the stages of personal growth we all pass through at various times in our lives, but they also highlight something else: our own personalities. Although we may, at certain times in our life and depending on the situation, each take on elements of all the court cards, at our core, we are most closely aligned to one of the cards. Are we the Romantic Adventurer following our heart wherever it leads? The Fearless Trailblazer, charging ahead with bold ideas and unstoppable energy? The Tenacious Dreamer, holding fast to hope and imagination even when life gets tough? Or the Tireless Worker, steadfastly building a future through patience and perseverance?

Each personality brings its own gifts to the world, in the same way that each of us carries a unique combination of strengths, challenges, and dreams. There is no right way to move through life, only the path that belongs to us. The court cards of the tarot are not a judgement of who we are, but an invitation to honour it.

Whether you use this book to deepen your tarot readings, develop character profiles, or better understand yourself and others, it is designed to be a clear and usable reference whenever you are faced with one of the court cards in a reading.

Language

In traditional tarot decks, the Pages, Knights, and Kings are often depicted as men, while Queens are depicted as women. However, in this book, I have chosen to present the court cards in a gender-neutral way.

Rather than using "he" or "she," I refer to each card's energy as "they." This allows for a more inclusive approach, recognising that the qualities and lessons of each court card transcend gender.

Whether you see yourself reflected in a Page, a Knight, a Queen, or a King, these archetypes speak to the spirit within, not the outward form.

The Four Characters

The tarot court comprises four distinct roles: Pages, Knights, Queens, and Kings. These roles offer insight into how we navigate the world, make decisions, and interact with others.

Pages represent curiosity, learning, and potential. They are the apprentices of the tarot, eager to explore, discover, and embrace new experiences. Pages are driven by a sense of wonder; the world is in front of them as a vast landscape to be explored. They symbolise the beginning of a journey filled with enthusiasm and a desire to grow.

Knights are the action-takers who pursue goals with intensity, passion, and purpose. They are the seekers, the adventurers who test their ideas, confront challenges, and blaze new paths. Knights charge boldly ahead, though they may not always pause to think things through. They represent drive, courage, and the will to achieve, no matter the cost.

Queens are deeply connected to their values and the needs of others. They embody care, compassion, and intuition, offering guidance and support. Their behaviour is based on understanding, empathy, and insight, making them the beating heart of their suit. They represent emotional maturity and can create environments where growth and harmony can flourish.

Kings bring knowledge, leadership, and strategic thinking. They guide others with clarity and confidence. Kings are visionaries and planners, bringing structure and ensuring that things function smoothly and efficiently. Their decisions are informed by wisdom, and they can use their resources; people, time, or money, to bring tangible results.

The Four Suits

There are four suits in the tarot: Cups, Pentacles, Swords and Wands. Each suit in the tarot guides the energy and influence of its court cards.

The Suit of Cups reflects emotions and intuition. Those aligned with Cups are often sensitive, empathetic, and in touch with their feelings. This suit teaches us the importance of emotional expression, but it can also bring a tendency to become overly introspective.

The Suit of Pentacles is focused on the material world, practicality, and security. Those aligned with Pentacles are grounded, dependable, and hardworking. This suit teaches us the importance of patience, stability, and long-term planning, but it can also lead to too much focus on material success at the expense of emotional fulfilment.

The Suit of Swords is based around logic. Those connected to Swords are sharp thinkers, strategic planners, and problem-solvers. This suit calls for clarity, truth, and rationality, though it can lead to overthinking or detachment if not balanced with empathy.

The Suit of Wands personifies passion, action, and creativity. Those aligned with Wands are often energetic, enthusiastic, and forward-thinking. They seek to create, explore, and push boundaries. The energy of Wands is bold and dynamic, but it can also lead to impulsiveness or restlessness if not kept in check.

The Tarot Court

Each court card offers a distinct personality, a unique voice within the tarot deck that reflects how we and others approach life, love, work, and personal growth. As you read through the sixteen descriptions on the following pages, take notice which ones feel familiar, which challenge you, and which spark recognition. You may find yourself in one card more than the others, or see aspects of your journey across several. There's no right or wrong way to live or behave and this book doesn't suggest there is, there are just insights to help you better understand yourself and the people around you.

The Court of Cups
The Page of Cups

The Tenacious Dreamer

The Page of Cups represents the childlike spirit of discovery. They see the world like a child would, with curious eyes and a heart open to new opportunities. This is the personality of someone who seeks beauty in every experience and listens closely to their innermost desires when making decisions and choices.

The Page of Cups navigates life through feelings and imagination. They are sensitive, often deeply empathic, and attuned to emotional undercurrents that others might miss. They see potential where others may only see possibilities. To the Page of Cups, life is a canvas for dreams, and they are both artist and muse.

Their creative spark often leads them into artistic pursuits or imaginative careers. They are drawn to poetry, music, and storytelling, where they can express what is in their soul to the outer world. Yet, this openness can also make them vulnerable; they have laid bare their innermost feelings to the world, and if the world doesn't like what it sees, they may retreat into themselves. They take criticism and obstacles personally and can disappear into themselves when faced with them. Despite this, they can remain resilient, and after a while, when they have had the chance to lick their wounds, they return to what they love with a sense of optimism that this time will be different. Nothing can dim the light that shines within the Page of Cups for long.

Core Traits

- Willing to explore their own feelings and is genuinely interested in understanding the emotions of others.
- Hold lofty ideals and visions for what life could be. Though this sometimes leads to disappointment when reality doesn't match their dreams, it also makes them a source of hope and inspiration to others.
- Feels things deeply and may need to guard their emotional boundaries. Their sensitivity is both a gift and a challenge; it connects them deeply to life but can leave them vulnerable.
- Trust in love and kindness and are often the first to extend a hand of friendship or forgiveness.

Strengths

- Natural empathy and compassion.
- Creative expression of emotions.
- Inspiring idealism that uplifts others.
- Openness to love, connection, and new emotional experiences.

Challenges

- Can be too trusting of people and situations.
- Tendency toward emotional naivety.
- Can fall into escapism when reality feels too harsh.
- Struggles with self-doubt and sensitivity to criticism.

Life Lessons

The Page of Cups is here to learn how to keep their dreams alive whilst navigating the practicalities of life. Their journey involves discovering how to let their dreams inspire them without becoming too lost in them, to keep their feet on the ground even though their heads may be in the clouds. Learning to trust their inner voice while discerning when to protect their tender heart is one of their lifelong lessons.

Relationships

In relationships, the Page of Cups is a gentle and romantic partner. They yearn for deep and meaningful connections, and once they have found it may idolise their loved ones, seeing them through rose-tinted glasses. They can accept flaws which others may not be so tolerant of. Their emotional availability can be healing, but they must be careful not to lose themselves in the feelings of others and allow others to guide their way. They thrive with partners who respect their sensitivity and nurture their creative spirit.

Career and Purpose

The Page of Cups excels in fields where empathy, creativity, and emotional intelligence are valued. They may be drawn to the arts, becoming artists, writers, or poets, or they may take on roles as counsellors, therapists, support workers, or teachers where they can inspire and help others find their purpose. They are motivated not by status or material success but by the pursuit of meaning and beauty in their work.

THE KNIGHT OF CUPS

THE ROMANTIC ADVENTURER

The Knight of Cups constantly searches for emotional experiences. Unlike the Page, who dreams of possibilities, the Knight pursues them boldly, driven by the mission to find beauty, love, and meaning in life. This is a person who follows the call of their heart wherever it may lead.

The Knight of Cups is a warrior, guided in their quest for passion by ideals and imagination. For them, in their chase for dreams, the journey is often more important than the destination, so they can often be discontented with what they have when they find it. They always want more. As individuals, they are magnetic and draw people to them with a natural, effortless charm. People are captivated by their romantic energy and sincerity of purpose.

Beneath their charismatic exterior, though, lies a deeply sensitive soul who feels life intensely. Though they may live in the moment, each moment means something special to them. They thrive on emotional experiences, whether these are in love, creativity, or spiritual exploration, and often see life as an ongoing quest for connection. Their passion fuels their actions, but can also make them restless, always searching for the next spark that ignites their love for life and captures their attention.

The Knight of Cups is not afraid to take risks, embark on adventures, and follow visions that others might dismiss as fanciful. Dreams are worth chasing in their world, even at the cost of comfort or certainty.

However, this same impulsive passion can sometimes lead them astray, pursuing elusive or unsustainable ideals.

Core Traits

- Always chasing the ideal, the Knight of Cups believes in true love, meaningful connections, and the beauty that can be found at the heart of everything.
- Their emotional enthusiasm is infectious. They have a way of inspiring others to join them on their adventures.
- Doesn't shy away from emotional risks. They bravely expose their heart in pursuit of love and creative expression.
- Live in pursuit of new adventures, whether romantic, artistic, or spiritual.

Strengths

- Inspires others with vision and charm.
- Courageous in their pursuit of emotional fulfilment.
- Romantic and expressive.
- Emotionally sincere and authentic.

Challenges

- Can chase illusions or romantic fantasies.
- Struggles with commitment, always seeking the next dream.
- Prone to mood swings if ideals are unmet.
- May neglect practicalities in pursuit of adventure.

Life Lessons

The Knight of Cups needs to learn to balance romantic idealism with the wisdom that fairytales are only found in books. Their journey through life is about discovering that meaning exists not just in the pursuit, but in the real, imperfect moments of connection.

Relationships

A passionate and attentive partner, the Knight of Cups loves deeply. They express affection through words and bold gestures. For them, passion is an essential element of romance.

However, their restless spirit means they can crave emotional variety and excitement; routine can feel stifling to them. They thrive with partners who share their enthusiasm for life, who are open to new experiences, and who are unafraid to explore all that love has to offer. When their romantic expressions are met with appreciation and reciprocation, the Knight of Cups feels truly alive and inspired to continually kindle the flames of connection.

Career and Purpose

Conventional, routine jobs rarely satisfy the Knight of Cups, and they are drawn to roles in the arts, healing, or any field that allows creative expression and emotional depth. The Knight of Cups seeks work that stirs their soul. Their natural empathy suits them for counselling, therapy, or holistic healing careers, where they can offer emotional insight and support. They may also be found in roles such as event planning, travel, or cooking, where they can create extraordinary experiences for others. Motivated by passion rather than pragmatism, they thrive when their work feels like an adventure and where each task feels like a journey.

The Queen of Cups

The Gentle Caregiver

The Queen of Cups is a still, peaceful presence at the centre of a world that can often be in turmoil and conflict. Like the eye of a storm, they radiate power, not through dominance or loud displays, but through simply being there. They offer a safe harbour for those needing solace, the trusted confidante, the one people instinctively turn to when life feels uncertain, and trouble is brewing. Their intuition is a finely tuned instrument, sensing what lies beneath the surface long before words are spoken. They listen not only with their ears but with their entire being, hears as much what is not said as what is said, and sees what is not shown as well as what can be seen. With a gentle word, a knowing glance, or simply the warmth of their presence, they can bring relief, validation, or encouragement, often saying or doing exactly what is needed at the right moment. Even if it is just a shoulder to cry on when that is what is needed most.

Unlike the energy of the Knight, who actively pursues emotional experiences, the Queen of Cups turns their energy inwards, drawing strength from that which lies within their own being. They do not chase feelings or connections but invites them to unfold naturally. They wait to be welcomed or asked rather than imposing themselves where they think they are needed. The Queen of Cups has a quiet strength that willingly draws people towards them, but they are as comfortable alone as they are in company. They do not need others to validate their self-worth. They are in control of their emotions, not through suppression or over-analysis, but through simply accepting they are who they are. The Queen of Cups can feel deeply without being overwhelmed, loves generously without losing themselves, and nurtures others while maintaining healthy boundaries. Unlike others, their true strength lies not in what they have or can do, but simply in who they are.

Core Traits

- Possesses a strong inner knowing and trusts their gut feelings. Sensitive to emotional undercurrents.
- Offers comfort and emotional support to those around them.
- Expresses emotions through art, writing, or healing practices. Sees beauty in subtlety and depth.
- Understands the complexity of emotions and holds space for both joy and sorrow, letting them live within them side by side.

Strengths

- Deep emotional understanding.
- Healing and nurturing presence.
- Trusts and follows inner guidance.
- Supports others with genuine empathy.

Challenges

- Can become emotionally immersed in the feelings of others.
- Prone to emotional overwhelm if boundaries aren't maintained.
- Tendency toward self-sacrifice.
- Needs solitude to recharge but may neglect this need.

Life Lessons

The Queen of Cups' life lesson is to learn how to surrender to the flow of life while maintaining their inner purpose. Though they may be the caregiver to others they must also nurture their own wants and needs, living authentically, keeping in mind that providing support to others does not mean sacrificing what they themselves need.

Relationships

The Queen of Cups is a deeply loyal and nurturing partner, offering not just affection but sanctuary. They create a safe space within their relationships, where both they and their partner can be seen, heard, and valued without fear of judgment. They often sense their partners needs before they are spoken. Their love runs deep and true, flowing beneath the surface with quiet intensity. They do not seek superficial bonds; rather, deep, meaningful connections that nourish and last.

Career and Purpose

The Queen of Cups is naturally drawn to a career that allows them to care for others and create environments of emotional well-being. They flourish in roles where their empathy and intuition are assets, such as nursing, counselling, teaching, eldercare, and childcare. Wherever there is a need for compassion, gentleness, and emotional support, the Queen of Cups feels at home.

But their calling is not limited to direct caregiving. The Queen of Cups is also drawn to crafting and creating and maintaining spaces of beauty and emotional resonance, such as art therapy, interior design, event management, libraries, museums, and galleries, anywhere they can create an experience for others that supports their emotional needs. For the Queen of Cups, the purpose lies in emotional enrichment, in helping others feel safe, seen, and soothed.

The King of Cups

The Compassionate Guide

The King of Cups represents emotional leadership; not only have they talked the talk but they have walked the walk as well. They can therefore be seen as a compassionate guide who has weathered life's storms, learned to navigate them with grace and lived not only to tell the tale but to show others the way. They stand, not as one untouched by feeling, but as someone deeply acquainted with the depths of human suffering and emotional turmoil. Their experiences have taught them that emotional turbulence is not a weakness to be feared but a force to be understood and channelled constructively for the good of others.

The King of Cups leads with empathy and governs with high emotional intelligence, offering calm and steady counsel even when those around them are determined to go their own way. Their presence is a safe harbour for others, and people are naturally drawn to their quiet strength and compassionate perspective. Yet, others should not be fooled into thinking the King of Cups is not tough; they have a spine of steel and a heart that, though filled with love, is surrounded by iron. They do not suffer fools at all, never mind gladly, and though they will show the way, they will not walk the path for others. They understand that they can only do so much to help others and can disconnect their emotions if others are not prepared to follow their lead and end up in difficulty.

A crucial part of the King of Cups' wisdom lies in their commitment to their own values. Though they may tend to the emotional needs of others, they will not shoulder the weight of their responsibility and will stay anchored to their own principles. They are acutely aware that their own strength comes from honouring their own personal convictions because it is then that they become an authentic and trustworthy guide for others.

The King of Cups teaches us that strength is not the absence of vulnerability but the courage to embrace it with integrity. By remaining true to their heart, even amidst the demands of the external world which often values a different path, they offer a powerful example of how compassion and conviction can coexist, guiding others with sincerity, balance, and inner purpose.

Core Traits

- Has learned to navigate emotional highs and lows with grace. Their calm presence soothes those in turmoil.
- Uses emotional intelligence to guide decisions and support others. Leads with the heart as well as the mind.
- Acts as a guardian of emotional well-being for their family, community, or team.
- Handles conflicts with empathy, striving for harmony and understanding.

Strengths

- Emotional intelligence and maturity.
- Steady, calming presence.
- Inspires trust and loyalty.
- Wise counsel and fair leadership.

Challenges

- Can repress personal feelings to maintain composure.
- Risk of emotional detachment if feels others are not following their lead.
- May carry others' burdens at the expense of self-care.
- Struggles with internalising stress.

Life Lessons

The life journey of the King of Cups revolves around the delicate balance between responsibility and authenticity. They are naturally cast in the role of the emotional protector; the one others turn to for support, stability, and wise counsel. Yet, in always being there for others, there is a temptation to suppress their own true feelings and emotional needs and to try to become someone they are not.

The King of Cups' life lesson is to recognise that guiding others towards their purpose does not require them to deny their own weaknesses. In fact, it is this willingness to acknowledge their own vulnerability and needs that makes them a more compassionate and effective guide. When others can see the whole journey that they have been on, it allows them to lay bare their own doubts and fears, be honest about what they want, and get the support they need.

Relationships

The King of Cups is a deeply loyal and generous partner, offering not only affection but also emotional stability to those they love. They become the anchor in their relationships, someone who can be relied upon through life's highs and lows. Their steady presence creates a safe and nurturing space where loved ones feel truly seen, heard, and valued.

However, while the King of Cups is naturally inclined to be the anchor for others, they also need to learn that intimacy thrives when they allow themselves to be vulnerable too. When they share their own feelings and open their heart fully, their relationships blossom into true partnerships, where both partners can give and receive support in equal measure. This takes time though to manifest, and any partners need to give the time and space to allow this to happen, for the risk is that relationships can end up being one-sided if this is not recognised or acted upon.

Career and Purpose

The King of Cups tends to be called to careers where emotional intelligence and compassionate guidance are paramount. They naturally thrive in roles such as counselling, psychotherapy, teaching, mentoring, and guiding others through emotional or life challenges. They have empathy and an intuitive understanding of human nature and can excel at helping people navigate the challenges of life.

They often feel drawn to charitable work and community leadership, particularly in organisations that serve the vulnerable and overlooked. This may include supporting prisoners on their path to rehabilitation, assisting those struggling with addiction, or advocating for those who need support that cannot be found in obvious places. Their steady, nonjudgmental presence can be a lifeline for many, and they are adept at guiding those who need help to find what they are looking for, even if they don't at first know what they are looking for or want to find it.

THE COURT OF PENTACLES
THE PAGE OF PENTACLES

THE AMBITIOUS LEARNER

The Page of Pentacles is the apprentice of the tarot court, someone who is just beginning their journey but already carries the seeds of future success. They embody the spirit of someone who not only dreams, and dreams big, but is ready to do the work to bring those dreams to life. With their feet planted firmly on the ground, they are practical, patient, and quietly determined to master their craft, whatever form it may take.

The Page of Pentacles sees learning as a long-term investment, and their ambition is not flashy or impulsive; it's measured, deliberate, and enduring. Whether pursuing a new field of study, committing to a skill, or taking the first steps toward financial independence, the Page of Pentacles is prepared to start at the bottom and build steadily upward. They understand that to master their craft, they must not only take the time to learn and understand but repeat the same steps many times over until they have mastered whatever it is they are determined to do.

As apprentices, they thrive when they have something tangible to work with, a plan, a routine, or a goal. They are not afraid of slow progress because they know every effort, however small, is a step along the path to their future. The Page of Pentacles respects time and understands that life is a marathon not a sprint. They are willing to grow from the ground up, slowly and deliberately turning knowledge into action and ideas into results.

Core Traits

- Eager to absorb useful, real-world knowledge and apply it in meaningful ways.
-
- Thinks beyond the present moment, often weighing actions by their long-term benefits and the stability they can bring.
- Resilient and accepts that though progress may be steady, it is always enduring.
- Holds onto big hopes and ideals but stays rooted in what is realistic and achievable.

Strengths

- Hardworking and dependable.
- Patient and methodical.
- Values growth and self-improvement.
- Loyal and trustworthy.

Challenges

- Can be overly cautious.
- Slow to adapt to change.
- Risks getting stuck in routine.
- Tends to undervalue intuition.

Life Lessons

The Page of Pentacles understands that building dreams is less about chasing success and more about creating it, one step, one task, one lesson at a time. They know that ambition alone is not enough; it must be matched by patience, persistence, and the willingness to adapt when things change.

The Page of Pentacles begins with a plan and a goal, but over time, needs to learn that true growth doesn't always follow a straight path. Detours, delays, and distractions are not failures, they are part of the path to learning. Their life lesson is to remain rooted in their values while staying open to new methods, ideas, and perspectives.

They must also learn to balance diligence with curiosity. When too focused on the result, they may miss the lessons that come with the journey itself. Flexibility becomes the key, allowing them to evolve without losing sight of what they're working toward.

Relationships

In relationships, the Page of Pentacles brings sincerity and loyalty. They may be cautious at the beginning of a relationship, taking their time to build trust, but once committed, they become steady and dependable. Their love is practical, expressed through small actions and thoughtful gestures, and there is a genuine desire to build a shared life rooted in stability.

This is someone who believes that relationships, like any worthwhile goal, require patience, effort, and communication. Once committed to a partner, they are prepared to work to make the relationship successful and appreciate partners who can match their efforts with their own. For the Page of Pentacles, mutual support is not just important; it is vital.

The problem for the Page of Pentacles, though, is that they can sometimes see love through the same lens as work, and their desire to put in the work to make it a success can come across as transactional. They need to learn that love isn't something to be mastered or measured but to be enjoyed and experienced. Letting go of rigid expectations and the pursuit of perfection and embracing emotional spontaneity will allow relationships to flourish more fully.

Career and Purpose

The Page of Pentacles is drawn to fields where growth is tangible, and hard work leads to visible, lasting results. They often gravitate toward careers in trades, whether working with their hands in trades like carpentry, pottery, gardening, or building, or refining their skills in more academic or technical fields such as research or engineering. What matters most to the Page of Pentacles is the opportunity to build something real and valuable, step by step.

They are natural apprentices eager to soak up knowledge and apply it in their work. Their practical mindset and patience allow them to thrive in environments others might find too slow or detail heavy. They are most fulfilled when they can work toward long-term goals, whether mastering a profession, developing a new skill, or creating a business from the ground up.

Purpose for the Page of Pentacles lies in steady growth not sudden, overnight success. They believe that life is not just about reaching the destination but about becoming someone wiser and more capable along the way.

The Knight of Pentacles

The Tireless Worker

The Knight of Pentacles is the protector of the material world, not only of what has been built but also the dreams of what is to come. This is the rancher who tends the land day in and day out, the ranger who patrols the fields and forests to protect them from hunters and poachers, and the farmer who rises with the sun, sowing seeds for future harvests. Slow and methodical, yet determined and strong-willed, this Knight can be found where courage, consistency, and responsibility are required.

The Knight of Pentacles is not here for glory or recognition. Their reward lies in fulfilled duty, tasks done right, and responsibilities taken care of quietly and without fuss. Where other knights may charge ahead or follow dreams, the Knight of Pentacles stays the course. They honour commitments, safeguard the well-being of others, and understand that real progress is rarely dramatic; it's incremental and forged through perseverance and dedication to the cause.

The Knight of Pentacles possesses a quiet strength. They are deeply loyal, slow to trust, but unwavering once they do. Their values are rooted in tradition, and their heart is tied to the land, the craft, or the cause they serve. We may not see their impact in a single moment but look back and we will see that they were the ones who held everything together when everyone else was losing their heads.

Core Traits

- Upholds their word with quiet strength, showing up consistently for others and earning deep respect over time.
- Takes a steady, step-by-step approach to challenges, understanding that true progress is built through persistence and care.
- Pays close attention to detail, ensuring that everything is done thoroughly and to a high standard.
- Stays connected to what's realistic and achievable, turning visions into results through hands-on effort and clear thinking.

Strengths

- Dependable and reliable.
- Steadfast under pressure.
- Disciplined work ethic.
- Values long-term stability.

Challenges

- May resist change or innovation.
- Risks overworking.
- Can seem slow or plodding.
- Tends toward rigidity.

Life Lessons

The Knight of Pentacles needs to learn that while steadiness can be noble if we are to grow and progress as we move through life, we sometimes must take risks and walk into the unknown. Although comfortable with what is proven and what works, life has a habit of calling us beyond the familiar and testing us with challenges we have not encountered before. The Knight's lesson is to trust that the same qualities that have made them dependable in what is known will serve them just as well when being asked to step into unfamiliar territory.

There is a fine line between staying firm and being immovable. The Knight of Pentacles must travel this line carefully, learning that not every task, action or success can be planned down to the last detail. There is wisdom in careful preparation but also strength in accepting that we must adapt. When the Knight of Pentacles lets go of the need for absolute certainty, they find that their steady nature can carry them across even uncharted ground.

Relationships

Loyal and dependable, the Knight of Pentacles is a partner who shows love through action. You won't always hear grand declarations from them, but you'll see it in the small, consistent things, showing up when it matters, following through on promises, and building a shared life with care and intention. They are someone who creates safety through presence and reliability.

Their approach to romantic relationships is much like everything else they do: with steady effort. This is someone who doesn't rush into love but is deeply committed once they're in. However, their tendency toward routine and practicality can sometimes make relationships feel overly structured. They may struggle with spontaneity or expressing emotions in a free-flowing way, which can leave more emotionally expressive partners craving warmth or variety. Above all though, the Knight of Pentacles is someone you can count on, a rock in times of change, and a safe place in an uncertain world.

Career and Purpose

The Knight of Pentacles excels in careers that reward persistence, structure, and long-term dedication. They are not drawn to flashy roles or overnight success; their fulfilment comes from putting in a steady effort and watching things grow over time. Whether tending to the land, managing projects, or safeguarding resources, their work is driven by duty and responsibility.

The Knight of Pentacles can often be found in roles like farming, conservation, park ranger, land management, and logistics, any role that demands patience, endurance, and care for systems or the natural world. They might also be drawn to protective or service-based roles such as security, health and safety, or emergency response, where others depend on their reliability.

Artisanry, engineering, and infrastructure, where precision and practicality are paramount, also suit them well. They may not seek leadership for its own sake, but others naturally trust them with responsibility because of their grounded nature and consistency.

The Queen of Pentacles

The Devoted Steward

The Queen of Pentacles blends a caregiver's nurturing spirit with a provider's practical mindset, creating a life of stability, comfort, and quiet abundance, not just for themselves but for all those they hold dear. They are the devoted steward of both home and land, a guardian of well-being, beauty, and balance. To them, a garden in bloom, a well-cooked meal, and the laughter of loved ones hold more meaning than gold. Deeply connected to nature, they understand that abundance lies not in material wealth, but in good health and living in harmony with the world. Although material wealth can come and go, the joy found in nature and community is ever-present. Their world is stewardship and guardianship, caring and nurturing what is important; they grow things, tend to what matters, and support others when they feel lost. To the Queen of Pentacles, the richness of life is measured by the love we give and the beauty we appreciate and protect in our surroundings. Stewardship, for them, is not just responsibility, it is duty.

This queen is not flashy, but they are formidable. They manage homes, businesses, and hearts with unwavering devotion, offering warmth and sanctuary in everything they touch. They provide a safe and stable presence, grounding those around them with calm reassurance and practical wisdom. Their power lies not in domination but in their ability to make others feel seen, supported, and safe. They teach through example, showing how to honour the land and build a life of quiet richness from the inside out.

Core Traits

- Creates safe, supportive spaces where others feel seen, heard, and cared for.
- Approaches life with a calm, level-headed perspective.
- Takes pride in being someone others can depend on. Ensures the needs of family, friends or community are thoughtfully and sustainably met.
- Stands firm in defence of those they love and the principles they hold dear.

Strengths

- Warm and supportive.
- Excellent at managing resources.
- Patient and caring.
- Keen sense of duty.

Challenges

- Risks over-giving.
- Can neglect their own needs.
- May fear there is not enough to go around, leading to over-giving or over-committing.
- Tends toward overprotection.

Life Lessons

The Queen of Pentacles must learn that their desire to look after others must also include themselves. While they instinctively provide; offering time, energy, and resources freely, their true lesson lies in understanding that their own well-being is not a luxury but a necessity. The hearth they keep burning for others must also warm their own spirit.

When they honour their need for rest and pleasure, they not only restore themselves but enhance their capacity to give. In time, they realise that true stewardship begins within. The same care they offer the world; to gardens, homes, and communities must be extended to their bodies, dreams, and peace of mind.

Relationships

The Queen of Pentacles brings warmth, loyalty, and care to their relationships. They are rocks, offering their loved ones a sense of home, not just physically but emotionally. Their love is expressed not just in words but in thoughtful details; a meal prepared with love, a comforting touch, a space made beautiful and safe.

The Queen of Pentacles seeks lasting, stable partnerships built on mutual support and shared values. Their devotion to their partner is strong, and they take real pride in being a dependable presence through life's difficulties. They are the ones who make everything in life seem a little more manageable. However, they must be mindful not to overextend themselves in caring for others at the expense of their own emotional needs. Relationships are built on harmony, not giving their all.

Careers and Purpose

The Queen of Pentacles thrives in careers where stewardship is expressed through practical means. They may be drawn to professions in holistic health, nutrition, herbalism, gardening, midwifery, or community-centred work. Unlike the Queen of Cups, whose care is deeply emotional and personal, the Queen of Pentacles supports in a physical sense.

They may find work as a carer of land or animals, someone who sees beauty and value in tending to what others might overlook. Roles in sustainable agriculture, eco-activism, and home design also reflect their instinct to create beauty and order in the physical world. As a natural steward of resources, they are also suited to financial planning and property management. Whether they manage a household, run a business, or support their community, their purpose is to make the material world more supportive, beautiful, and balanced for everyone.

THE KING OF PENTACLES

THE PROSPEROUS PATRON

The King of Pentacles epitomises material success and wealth creation, grounded in a deep understanding of value and long-term stability. They know how to build a legacy, not through quick gains, but reliable, sustainable growth. Like a wise investor, they understand the importance of patience and the rewards of carefully tending to what they value. Whether in business, relationships, or personal ventures, the King of Pentacles applies their steady hand and a sharp eye for detail to every endeavour, always mindful of what's best for the future.

They have a refined understanding of the true meaning of success, seeing beyond surface-level wealth to the deeper value of legacy and the impact they can have on others. Whilst focused on business or investments, the King of Pentacles also has a deep sense of responsibility for those they support. They know that true prosperity isn't simply about accumulation but also creating opportunities for others.

At their core is their ability to plan meticulously, avoid impulsive decisions, and steadily build toward the future with a reliable hand. Their success stems not from immediate rewards but from a vision that takes time to materialise, and they remain deeply committed to sustaining that vision, knowing that what they create will endure for generations. Their role in any situation is to lead with quiet authority, providing inspiration and tangible support to those around them.

Core Traits

- Understands that true prosperity isn't just about acquiring wealth, but about building something lasting.
- Leads by example. People trust them because they deliver on their promises and remain calm under pressure.
- Focuses on what works in the real world. Values real-world outcomes over lofty ideals.
- Takes pride in being a provider. Uses their strength and resources to shelter and support others, although their care may be expressed more through action than emotion.

Strengths

- Exceptional provider.
- Practical decision-maker.
- Reliable and trustworthy.
- Creates stability and prosperity.

Challenges

- May prioritise practical or material success over emotional connection.
- Risks defaulting to traditional approaches over new ways or working.
- Can resist innovation.
- Struggles with vulnerability.

Life Lessons

The King of Pentacles' journey is about understanding that prosperity becomes meaningful and lasting when it is shared. True success lies not in what they have but in what they do with it, whether through investing in others, mentorship, charitable acts, or creating opportunities for those in their circle.

While the King of Pentacles is an expert at building wealth and securing a stable foundation, their most important lesson is balancing this drive for success with the need to contribute to the greater good. Through this process, the King of Pentacles comes to realise that security and abundance are tools for empowering others. When this success is used to support the community, they experience a deeper sense of fulfilment. Wealth is not just about what is possessed but about how it is used to create a lasting, positive impact on the future.

Relationships

In relationships, the King of Pentacles values stability and security and seeks to create a foundation of trust and reliability for their loved ones.

Their approach to love and partnership is grounded in practical love; they show affection through actions rather than romantic gestures. Whether it's taking care of the immediate household needs, or working all hours to provide for the future, their love is often demonstrated through practical support. They are a dependable partner who can be counted on through both calm and storm.

However, the King of Pentacles' intense focus on providing and creating a secure environment for others can sometimes make them appear distant or overly focused on work, as they may prioritise tangible outcomes over emotional connection. They may struggle to express their emotions verbally, believing that actions speak louder than words. This can lead to emotional distance, even though they are deeply invested in the well-being of those they love.

Career and Purpose

The King of Pentacles thrives in roles where their natural ability to create and manage wealth and provide stability can shine. They are drawn to positions of power and responsibility, where their leadership, practical skills, and long-term vision are highly valued. Whether in business, finance, or entrepreneurship, this is the type of person who can build empires.

They excel in roles that require solid judgment, financial acumen, and long-term planning. The King of Pentacles may find fulfilment as a CEO, investor, or management consultant, where they can put their skills to work creating sustainable success. In a more practical sense, they may also be drawn to careers that require hands-on expertise, such as farming or construction, where they can use their resourcefulness and meticulous attention to detail to build and maintain something tangible and lasting. The King of Pentacles' goal is to create security and prosperity, not only for themselves, but also their community and future generations. They believe that a career is a vehicle through which they can manifest abundance and leave a legacy that endures far beyond their lifetime.

The Court of Swords
The Page of Swords

The Quick Thinker

The Page of Swords embodies curiosity in motion. They have a restless mind and a desire to explore every idea, question every assumption, and uncover every secret. This is the youthful spirit of intellect and inquiry, always seeking something new to learn. They are the inquisitive thinkers, the constant questioners, the ones who challenge what's known to discover what might be.

But with such an agile intellect comes a temptation to leap to conclusions too quickly because their minds work much quicker than situations, circumstances and actions can evolve. The Page of Swords can snatch at a discovery and rush to act on it without pausing to reflect. Their mental energy is electric, but their challenge is to ground it in discernment.

The Page of Swords has a sharp wit, a quick comment, and a ready response. They love a debate but for the debate itself rather than to win, because winning is not important to them. It is the journey that is of interest, not the destination. They are lifelong learners and may take various positions over time as their view of the world constantly evolves, sometimes suddenly and without warning, as new insights arrive like flashes of lightening. This can catch people off guard, and others may question their consistency and loyalty, unsure whether the Page of Swords is committed or simply chasing the next interesting idea.

The Page of Swords' journey through life is about learning to wield their thoughts like a sword: not to slash indiscriminately but with skill, intention, and care. When they slow down enough to integrate what they know, the Page of Swords becomes not only clever but truly wise.

Core Traits

- Always asking "why?" and "how? Driven by a hunger to understand how things work beneath the surface.
- Notices details others overlook. Whether in conversations, studies, or situations, they spot inconsistencies and hidden insights with ease.
- Processes information quickly. They thrive in fast-paced environments where thinking on their feet is essential.
- Loves to share ideas and debate concepts.

Strengths

- Highly analytical.
- Quick-witted and perceptive.
- Open to new ideas.
- Passionate about learning.

Challenges

- Can be argumentative or overly critical.
- Impatient with slower thinkers.
- Risks intellectual arrogance.
- Restless mind, prone to distraction.

Life Lessons

The Page of Swords lesson is about understanding that life is not always about answers but rather asking the right questions. They need to know when to speak and when to listen, when to act and when to observe. With a mind that races ahead, they must learn the value of patience and the power of reflection if they are to truly make their mark on the world.

There is a tendency to leap to conclusions or make hasty decisions the moment something new is uncovered. While their quick thinking and sharp intellect can be a gift, they cannot fulfil their true potential if it is not grounded in the ability to understand and reflect. The Page of Swords succeeds most when they learn to research more thoroughly, and to trust that not every problem must be solved instantly. Wisdom, for them, lies in knowing when to press go and when to pause.

Relationships

In relationships, the Page of Swords brings lively conversation and a curious mind, interested in discovering all there is to know about their partner's thoughts and inner world. They are engaging and attentive, always asking questions and seeking to understand. They crave emotional stimulation more than anything else and are most fulfilled when with someone who can challenge their thinking and keep up with their ever-turning mind.

However, the risk can be that their quick wit and sharp observations can sometimes come across as blunt or overly critical, especially if they speak before fully considering the emotional impact of their words. Their restless nature can also make them seem inconsistent in their emotional presence, leading partners to feel unsure of where they stand. Trust and depth in relationships grow as the Page of Swords learns to listen as much as they speak, and to recognise that sometimes it is best to keep their mouth closed rather than open it and say what is on their mind.

Career and Purpose

With a sharp mind and an insatiable curiosity, the Page of Swords thrives in mentally stimulating and ever-evolving environments. They are natural researchers, analysts, writers, and communicators, always gathering information, connecting dots, and uncovering patterns others may overlook. Their gift lies in their ability to translate complex or disparate pieces of information into a cohesive whole, making sense of chaos and bringing clarity.

They are drawn to careers in journalism, academia, law, medicine, data analysis, investigative work, and education. They love roles where they can find things out, but their challenge is in staying focused and following through when the answers have been found. The Page of Swords tends to jump from project to project, propelled by initial excitement but quickly distracted by a new puzzle. Their growth comes from learning how to sustain interest through the slower phases of a task, and understanding that a job doesn't end with the first solution.

THE KNIGHT OF SWORDS

THE FEARLESS TRAILBLAZER

The Knight of Swords charges into life like a warrior, sword raised, mind sharp, and ideas blazing. The Knight of Swords is the archetype of someone who thrives on challenge, debate, and disrupting the status quo. They are bold, quick-thinking, and fearless, often seeing solutions to problems others have not yet defined.

With a keen sense of purpose and a belief that they are always right, and their way is the one everyone should take, the Knight of Swords is ready to champion their cause, defend their faith, and force through their beliefs. Sometimes, all at once, for they are not ones to let the grass grow under their feet if they believe in something. They are natural disruptors and reformers, unwilling to sit back when there's a fight worth having or a truth worth telling. Their words are weapons, and their ideas turn into change.

Yet for all their brilliance and conviction, the Knight of Swords can sometimes leap before looking, charging ahead without pausing to consider the ripple effects of their actions. They may dive headfirst into committing to a bold course of action before all the facts are in, swept along by adrenaline and certainty. What feels like decisive leadership to them may come across as reckless haste to others.

This tendency to jump in with both feet can lead to unnecessary conflict and actions that never fulfil their potential. Sometimes, they are their own worst enemy because the truth is risk and hard work are not always rewarded. Though their work ethic and passion for progress are unmatched, if something has not been well thought through at the beginning, it is destined to fail no matter how much energy is spent. But it is rare that the Knight of Swords will be too perturbed by failure, for they will just move on to the next idea.

They are endlessly curious and often on the move, chasing ideas and causes with a sense of urgency that others may find exhausting. Their high energy knows no bounds and is teamed with resilience and courage that enables them to make even the toughest challenge seem like a pebble on their path. They are the go-getters of the tarot court, bold, relentless, and unafraid to chase down their dreams, no matter how far away they may seem.

Core Traits

- Driven by conviction they fight fiercely for what they believe is right.
- Quick decision makers who acts with speed and certainty.
- Enjoys lively discourse and argument.
- Ambitious and competitive, loves intellectual and real-world challenges.

Strengths

- Fearless in pursuit of goals.
- Highly persuasive communicator.
- Strategic and analytical.
- Quick to adapt in fast-moving situations.

Challenges

- Can be impulsive and tactless.
- May rush into situations without fully knowing all the information.
- Struggles with patience.
- Can become combative.

Life Lessons

The Knight of Swords' lesson is to learn that speed and certainty do not always win the race of life. While their boldness and decisiveness are great assets, the Knight of Swords can sometimes act with such urgency that they overlook the full scope of a situation, rushing into decisions before all the facts are known. Their challenge is to recognise that patience isn't a weakness and that to wait is not a sign of indecision, but wisdom.

If the Knight of Swords is to fulfil their true potential, then they must learn the value of timing, to understand that even the most brilliant ideas need space to mature. When they can balance conviction with consideration and know when to charge ahead and when it is better to pause, listen, and reflect, they become a truly unstoppable force.

Relationships

In relationships, the Knight of Swords is direct, forthright, and straightforward. Any partner knows exactly where they stand with them. They also bring excitement and challenge, pushing conversations to deeper levels, testing boundaries, and encouraging their partner to grow, think, and evolve. Their honesty is refreshing, and they tend to approach love with the same determination they bring to all areas of their life.

However, this directness and the intensity in which it can manifest can sometimes be overwhelming. They may rush headlong into relationships without fully understanding what they or the other person needs and speak too bluntly before considering how their words might land. Patience and emotional nuance are skills they must cultivate if they want their partnerships to thrive.

The Knight of Swords thrives with partners who appreciate their drive but can help them slow down and reflect. With the right person, they become fiercely loyal and inspiring companions, one who brings energy, vision, and excitement to the shared journey of love.

Career and Purpose

The Knight of Swords excels in roles that require quick thinking, decisive action, and bold communication. They thrive in fast-paced environments where their mental agility and assertiveness can shine, such as journalism, law, technology innovation, project leadership, sales, and marketing, any role where their competitive streak and desire to move forward can be displayed.

With their fearless drive and ability to see the bigger picture, they are natural disruptors, challenging the status quo and charging towards a vision of a better future. They can also make good business leaders and entrepreneurs, but their tendency to act before fully planning means they benefit from collaborators who can help ground their ideas and refine their execution.

The Queen of Swords

The Discerning Judge

The Queen of Swords embodies the wisdom of clarity with the strength of conviction. They are not easily swayed by emotion or external influence, and once they have come to a judgement, they stand firm in their decisions with the assurance of someone who knows that they are right. Their sharp intellect coupled with their perception of what may be happening beneath the surface of a situation, what is unsaid as well as what is said, makes them an expert at cutting through the noise and the fluff and identifying precisely what is happening and what needs to be done.

In any situation, the Queen of Swords critically evaluates facts and weighs every detail before offering their verdict. Once the verdict has been given, it will not be changed. Their judgments are fair and based on truth and logic rather than personal feelings. Others admire them for the clarity they bring and the confidence with which they uphold their principles. When they speak, people listen.

The Queen of Swords represents the voice of reason; they can make tough decisions without flinching or worrying about what people think of them. There is real strength in their ability to detach when necessary, ensuring that their decisions are not clouded by personal bias or emotion. While others may falter on the altar of emotion, they remain unshaken by individual circumstances, both willing and able to speak their truth no matter what others may think.

Core Traits

- Insightful and perceptive, can see through falsehoods with ease.
- A clear communicator who expresses themselves with precision.
- Trusts their own intellect over popular opinion and doesn't worry what others may think of them.
- Holds themselves and others to exacting standards.

Strengths

- Exceptional clarity of thought.
- Honest and forthright.
- Deeply intuitive and wise.
- Excellent judgment.

Challenges

- Can appear cold or aloof.
- May be overly critical.
- Struggles to show vulnerability.
- Risks isolation.

Life Lessons

There is a fine line between discernment and dismissal, and The Queen of Swords may sometimes shut down opposing viewpoints too quickly, assuming they have already seen all there is to see. Their life lesson is to temper justice with empathy, to remain curious and compassionate even when they believe they are right because they are not infallible even though they may think they are.

Truth doesn't have to be harsh to be honest. When the Queen of Swords softens their edges, they may find that people are more willing to open up, and new layers of insight are revealed. Their true evolution lies not in sacrificing their standards but in realising that understanding what has led to another's path is just as important as the path itself.

When they do so, they become not just a judge of what is fair, but a guardian of fairness itself.

Relationships

The Queen of Swords brings honesty, clarity, and exacting standards in relationships. They are deeply loyal and expect the same in return, not through sentiment, but through mutual respect and integrity. With them, what you see is what you get; they do not play games, and they do not hide their feelings behind niceties or vague gestures. Their partner will always know where they stand, even if they may not be standing exactly where they want to be.

The Queen of Sword's communication style is direct, and while it may come across as blunt to some, it comes from a desire for truth, not cruelty. They value intellectual connection and meaningful dialogue, often preferring depth over drama. However, emotional intimacy can be challenging as they fear vulnerability and have learned to guard their heart tightly. For relationships to thrive, the Queen of Swords must learn to soften their edges and let others in, discovering that love can be based on emotion not logic and not every situation requires analysis.

Career and Purpose

The Queen of Swords thrives in careers that require a logical mind and an unwavering moral compass. These traits bring precision and ethical judgment to everything they do. Naturally drawn to roles in law, governance, and public policy, they excel in positions where integrity and structure are key.

Fields such as compliance, governance, and human resources are especially well-suited to them. In these areas, they can ensure that regulations and standards are followed and that both individuals and institutions are protected. As a compliance officer, HR director, governance consultant, or ethics board member, they are the ones who hold the line, unafraid to make difficult calls in service of the greater good.

Whatever path they choose, their true purpose lies in using their wisdom to bring clarity and justice. Their words carry weight, and their guidance creates spaces where words are not only spoken, but honoured.

The King of Swords

The Wise Architect

The Wise Architect of the tarot court, the King of Swords, is a commanding presence, not through emotional display or force, but through the sharp precision of their mind and the strength of their convictions. With logic as the cornerstone on which everything is built, they see the world like a blueprint, structured, layered, and full of potential to be realised. Every detail is considered, every connection deliberate, as they methodically shape their surroundings to reflect their vision of order and efficiency. Nothing is left to chance, and every step forward is a calculated move towards creating a more refined, balanced reality.

This is a figure who plans for the long term. Where others may be swayed by emotion or impulse, the King of Swords maintains a clear head to find the most rational course of action. Like an architect with a vision, they draw on knowledge and structure to create order, meticulously planning each phase and ensuring every element aligns with the bigger picture.

Yet, despite being governed by logic, not emotion, there is no coldness in their approach. While they may appear detached in their decision-making, often taking themselves away from the people they love to assess and decide on a course of action, they possess a quiet warmth and a genuine care for the well-being of others. Their ability to listen, analyse, and offer insightful guidance comes from a place of fairness and equality, not indifference, ensuring that whatever they do is effective and compassionate.

Core Traits

- Commands respect not through force, but through knowledge and clear reasoning.
- Thinks several steps ahead, mapping out long-term goals and designing practical pathways to reach them.
- Values fairness above all but doesn't let emotion cloud their judgement.
- Maintains focus under pressure. Their inner strength lies in their ability to remain rational, responsible, and true to their purpose.

Strengths

- Clear and logical thinker.
- Wise and judicious leader.
- Excellent problem-solver.
- Fair and principled.

Challenges

- May come across as detached.
- Risks over-intellectualising situations.
- Can suppress emotions.
- Struggles with flexibility.

Life Lessons

The King of Swords must learn that authority is not found in control or intellectual superiority, but in the ability to wield knowledge with care. While they may naturally seek order and clarity in the world around them, they must also understand that a life is not built on data and logic, but on the experiences that have shaped people, and the emotions that create the stories behind them.

For all their insightful brilliance, the King of Swords must learn to stay open to perspectives beyond their own mind and recognise that in building a future for others, others must also be allowed to contribute to the design. For it is only when their intellect is combined with that of others that their ideas and actions become a structure that stands the test of time.

Relationships

In relationships, the King of Swords offers loyalty and support. They may not be openly expressive partners, but their love is steadfast and grounded in respect and intellectual connection. Don't expect flowers or chocolates; the way they show they care is by offering guidance, creating stability, and being a consistent presence.

They value honesty and clear communication and expect the same in return. If arguments or disagreements occur, they will seek a resolution through dialogue. While their partner may sometimes long for more emotional expression, they'll never be left guessing where they stand. They know that they are loved, even though they sometimes may not feel loved.

As architects of the future, the King of Swords doesn't live in the moment. They seek to build a relationship that can grow and evolve over time. They are the type of partner who thinks long-term, laying strong emotional and practical foundations that allow a relationship to flourish for years to come. However, this tendency to intellectualise emotions can create distance if left unchecked, and it is down to any partner to show them that though logic and emotions are worlds apart, love can be a bridge that brings them together.

Career and Purpose

True to their title as the Wise Architect, the King of Swords is both a planner and a builder, not only of systems or institutions but of ideas, models, and movements. They may be a literal architect, or engineer, or a designer of policies, strategies, educational frameworks, or conceptual blueprints that shape the world around them. They think in layers, creating structures with purpose and longevity. For them, career success is not just measured in outcomes but in the elegance and integrity of the design itself.

The King of Swords often finds fulfilment in roles that allow them to design solutions that stand the test of time. Whether crafting legal frameworks, building knowledge systems, or mentoring future leaders, they find satisfaction and their calling when they are allowed to create order from confusion and complexity.

The Court of Wands

The Page of Wands

The Enthusiastic Campaigner

The Page of Wands is like the spark that ignites a wildfire; a soul bursting with uncontrolled, untamed enthusiasm and curiosity for all that life has to offer. With an unquenchable thirst for new experiences, they are the embodiment of youthful fire, always on the edge of discovery, ready to dive headfirst into new adventures. For the Page of Wands, life is not something to be feared or carefully measured; it is to be lived boldly, felt deeply, and pursued with passion.

The Page of Wands sees potential everywhere; in people, in projects, in places, and their excitement is infectious. They have a way of rallying others with their natural charisma and contagious sense of wonder. Even in the face of uncertainty or lack of experience they step forward with courage, trusting that the path will unfold before them before their feet touch the ground. Mistakes are not failures to them, but a natural and necessary part of learning all there is to know about themselves and life.

They are often drawn to causes and ideas that inspire their values and challenge the status quo. With their natural flair for communication and sense of justice, many Pages of Wands find themselves instinctively campaigning; whether standing up for what's right in their community, speaking out for those unheard, or throwing themselves into social and environmental causes with high degrees of energy.

The Page of Wands is a trendsetter; creative, idealistic, and fiercely independent, creating paths that others can follow. However, they are not searching for new adventures just for the thrill of the chase, although that is part of their mindset. They are guided by a sense of purpose that is still to take shape fully. Ultimately, the Page of Wands reminds us of the joy of new adventures, the spark of courage to start and the flame of passion that keeps the adventure alive.

Core Traits

- Lives for exploration, whether literal travel or intellectual discovery.
- Shares excitement and ideas freely, inspiring others.
- Sees possibilities everywhere.
- An optimistic risk taker who embraces the unknown with open arms.

Strengths

- Endless curiosity and creativity.
- Infectious energy.
- Open-minded and adaptable.
- Quick to seize new opportunities.

Challenges

- Can be impulsive and scattered.
- Loses interest quickly.
- Struggles with follow-through.
- Restless if not engaged.

Life Lessons

The Page of Wands is easily captivated by new ideas, but not all are meant to be pursued. Maturity comes when they pause long enough to ask the question: What truly matters to me?

The answer to that question allows them the time and energy to balance the first spark of passion and spontaneity with the intention to follow through on what is important and will create lasting change. It gives them the opportunity to build momentum purposefully without burning out. For fire does not need to flare chaotically to be strong.

Relationships

The Page of Wands is warm, vibrant, and full of life. They bring joy and adventure to relationships that keeps things fresh and exciting. Romantic at heart, they fall in love with possibilities, the idea of love, and the adventure of connection. They are often drawn to people who are like them, who inspire them, challenge them, and encourage them to try new things. Shared passions, hobbies, and spontaneous getaways are the language of love that they can instantly respond to and relate to.

However, their enthusiasm for what is new and exciting can sometimes lead them to move too quickly in matters of the heart. They tend to dive into relationships without fully grounding themselves. They may struggle with restlessness or wanderlust, especially if a relationship feels stagnant or overly predictable. For the Page of Wands to thrive in love, they need partners who support their freedom, understand their need for creative expression, and are willing to grow alongside them.

Career and Purpose

The Page of Wands thrives in roles that ignite their passion. They are natural starters, full of visionary ideas, creative enthusiasm, and the courage to leap where others hesitate. They tend to be drawn to fields that allow them to inspire change, such as activism and campaigning. They become unstoppable when they align their career with a cause they care about, or a vision they genuinely believe in. Their charisma and ability to speak from the heart make them compelling spokespeople and spirited organisers.

Entrepreneurship also appeals to their adventurous nature. Starting new ventures, launching creative projects, or trying untested ideas gives them a sense of purpose and excitement. They are the type to build something from scratch, often not for profit alone, but because they believe in the mission behind it. Even when resources are limited, their sheer enthusiasm opens doors and allows them to get what they want.

They may also be drawn to careers that involve travel, exploration, or sharing their stories, such as travel writing, being a tour guide, motivational speaking, or cultural exchange. They thrive in roles where no two days are the same, for the Page of Wands certainly isn't meant for confined or rigid work structures.

The Knight of Wands

The Bold Pioneer

The Knight of Wands is filled with dynamic energy, bravery, and courage, leading them to seek new horizons and constantly explore the world in front of them. With fire in their heart and a vision that refuses to be tamed, this archetype is always ready and willing to pursue a new challenge; to conquer the next goal, scale the next peak, or launch the next big idea. This bold pioneer lives for physical, mental, and spiritual movement and thrives in the space between inspiration and action.

Unlike the Knight of Cups, who seeks emotional fulfilment, the Knight of Wands is driven by a thirst for experience, progress, and personal power. They not only like to do but like to be seen to be doing. They are natural risk-takers, unafraid to step into the unknown if it promises growth or excitement. Fuelled by a passionate belief in their potential, they rarely wait for permission; they are the ones who make things happen.

The Knight of Wands rarely walks their path alone and can naturally attract others to their next challenge. Their confidence and spontaneity light fires in those around them, though they can sometimes burn too brightly, and once the challenge has been overcome, they can get bored and move on to the next big thing, leading others to finish what they have started. This tendency to rarely follow through can mean they never quite fulfil their potential and can give them a reputation for letting people down.

To the Knight of Wands, life is an epic journey meant to be lived out loud, with urgency and impact. Their story is one of breakthroughs and bold moves, but they need others to grow and maintain what they have begun.

Core Traits

- Courageous and bold, they leap into action and are unafraid of taking risks.
- Inspire others with infectious enthusiasm and a natural magnetism that rallies people to their cause.
- Needs meaningful challenges to feel alive, pouring energy into pursuits that ignite their inner fire.
- Always seeking new frontiers, they thrive on adventure and the thrill of breaking new ground.

Strengths

- Fearless and action-oriented.
- Natural leadership and charisma.
- High energy and motivation.
- Quick decision-making.

Challenges

- Impulsive and impatient.
- Can burn or fizzle out quickly.
- Overlooks details in haste.
- Struggles with consistency.

Life Lessons

The Knight of Wands is brilliant at launching ideas, inspiring change, and breaking new ground. But their greatest life lesson is learning the power of follow-through. While they love the thrill of the chase and the excitement of achievement, they can quickly lose interest once the goal is reached, eager to move on to the next adventure. They must learn that value lies not only in starting something but in staying with it to the end.

Sustained success requires more than action; it demands commitment to walking the less glamorous parts of a journey. For the Knight of Wands, the challenge is to balance their initial passion with patience to create a lasting impact.

Relationships

In love, the Knight of Wands tends to be passionate and spontaneous. They bring a sense of adventure to their relationships, the kind of partner who might plan a last-minute getaway or surprise you with a bold declaration of love and affection. Their enthusiasm can be contagious, and they thrive with partners who share their zest for life and can accept that they never truly know what will happen next.

This fiery, passionate nature can, though, lead to restlessness. The Knight of Wands may struggle with routine in a relationship, and they can become impatient and lose interest if a relationship begins to feel as though it is becoming stagnant. Their challenge is to recognise whilst love may start as a whirlwind, a relationship develops into a slow, steady flame.

Career and Purpose

The Knight of Wands thrives in fast-paced, high-energy careers where passion and persuasion are key. Naturally charismatic and confident, they excel in roles that require communication, persuasion, charm, and quick thinking, making them ideal for sales, marketing, advertising, and public relations roles. They even make good politicians. Whether launching a new brand, leading a campaign, or pitching to a crowd, the Knight of Wands is adept at inspiring and persuading others to take action and follow their lead.

They are the pioneers who aren't afraid to pitch big ideas and take risks. Their drive to make things happen means they often rise quickly in their chosen career. However, their challenge lies in staying the course once the initial excitement disappears, for the danger is that they can come across as all style and no substance if they don't. Careers that allow for constant innovation, movement, and variety will keep them working at their best, for they are not made for repetitive routines. They need work that excites their spirit and offers opportunities to break new ground. At their best, they become powerful change agents, at their worst a restless distractor.

The Queen of Wands

The Enduring Pillar

The Queen of Wands is filled with confidence, passion, and purpose, but there is also a steadiness to the Queen, which means that they never need to use force to get what they want. Instead, they have an inner strength and quiet conviction, which means they create a channel into which life flows in the direction they want. This can give the impression that what they want comes naturally to them, that they can automatically attract what they want to their life, but it is not that easy; the Queen of Wands just makes it look easy.

The Queen of Wands' purpose is rooted in humility, integrity, and an unwavering commitment to their responsibilities. They honour their commitments with consistency and, even in the face of adversity, hold themselves with poise and an unshakeable belief that they will get through it. Their presence in the lives of others calms, inspires, and commands respect, not because they demand it but because they embody it.

Unlike the Page's youthful impulsiveness or the Knight's daring ambition, the Queen of Wands has mastered the fire element of the wands. They do not have the risk of burning out or flickering, their controlled power sustains the flame so that it burns brightly and continuously. Their flame is one of endurance, guiding others through example. They not only know what they want but are deeply attuned to the needs of those around them.

The Queen of Wands often serves as their community's or family's backbone, the one people turn to for encouragement, wisdom, and strength. Their sense of self is rooted in service as much as self-expression. They teach us that personal power is not diminished by service but defined by it.

Core Traits

- Naturally charismatic and can draw people in with authenticity and warmth.
- Transforms inspiration into action, trusting their instincts and capabilities every step of the way.
- Builds others up, nurturing their potential. Encourages and empowers those around them, offering steadfast support and genuine belief in their abilities.
- Follows their path with courage and conviction, inspiring others to do the same.

Strengths

- Confident and self-assured.
- Inspires loyalty and admiration.
- Passionate and magnetic.
- Fearless in pursuit of goals.

Challenges

- Can be perceived as intimidating.
- Risks overextending themselves.
- May suppress vulnerability to maintain strength.
- Impatient with delays

Life Lessons

The Queen of Wands needs to learn that true strength is not in always having the answers or maintaining perfect composure, but in being unapologetically themselves. Their power does not come from being perfect, but from being present, in daring to be themselves and not who they believe others need them to be. Often finding themselves in roles of leadership or influence, they may feel the pressure to uphold an image of flawless control. Yet their greatest gift lies not in appearing untouchable but in allowing others to see their heart, in knowing that vulnerability doesn't weaken their authority but deepens it.

Relationships

The Queen of Wands is a passionate, generous, and intensely loyal partner. They bring warmth into their relationships and light up the lives of those around them with enthusiasm and encouragement. In love, they are both a best friend and a fierce ally. They champion their partner's dreams as wholeheartedly as they pursue their own, thriving in relationships where mutual respect, shared values, and a spark of adventure are present. They are not content with superficial connections but seek a partner who can match their depth, spirit, and purpose.

Though they may outwardly appear strong and independent, they need to be appreciated and valued for all that they do. Their challenge in relationships can be a tendency to take on too much or to downplay their own needs in favour of keeping everything running smoothly. They need to remember that true partnership is built on shared effort, not silent sacrifice.

Career and Purpose

The Queen of Wands thrives in roles where they inspire others and make a meaningful difference. Their career path is often guided by a keen sense of civic duty, a calling to serve their community and stand for something greater than themselves.

Careers in teaching, community leadership, social work, public service, and nonprofit advocacy often show their desire to give back and lead by example. They may also be found in roles that require public visibility and responsibility, perhaps standing in local elections or running a community charity. Though they are capable of extraordinary independence, their leadership is rarely about self-interest. It's about service with soul, combining ambition with altruism and vision with compassion.

THE KING OF WANDS

THE COURAGEOUS COMMANDER

As the Courageous Commander, the King of Wands strides through life with purpose, confidence, and a firm belief in their mission. They are the ones who get things done, rally others to the cause with conviction and determination, and drive them forward to achieve what needs to happen. No, is not a word they respond to or understand.

This is a personality that is, like steel, forged in fire. Shaped by challenge and tested by life, they are determined to leave a legacy. Where others hesitate, the King of Wands charges ahead, fuelled by a fierce inner drive and a deep trust in their instincts. They possess the rare gift of long-range vision paired with immediate action, seeing what is possible and doing what is necessary to bring it into being.

Unlike the Queen of Wands, who leads through service, the King leads through command. They tell rather than show, demand instead of asking. The irony is that although that is their natural style, they rarely have to use it. People follow their lead because they gravitate towards the powerful energy that emanates from them; they see the potential, the accomplishments, the success, and the victory, and they want to be part of that. The King of Wands is the Pied Piper of the tarot deck.

Core Traits

- A strategist who sees beyond current limitations to future possibilities.

- Leads with a strength and conviction that others find impossible to ignore.
- Dynamic and driven they channel passion into focused action that gets results.
- A natural leader who cares more about elevating others to meet their potential rather than their own place in the world.

Strengths

- Bold and visionary leadership.
- Courageous decision-making.
- Charismatic authority.
- Motivates teams to achieve greatness.

Challenges

- Can be over-dominant.
- Impatient with less driven personalities.
- Risks burnout from relentless pursuit of goals.
- May struggle with delegation.

Life Lessons

With great power comes responsibility, and for the King of Wands, the responsibility is to lead with compassion. The lesson for the King of Wands is that though they are driven by a deep-rooted sense of purpose, that sense of purpose does not necessarily reside in others. Others can be shown the way they can take, but must not be driven there by force, they can be shown what they can do and what they can bring but cannot be made to do it. Desire and determination can achieve remarkable things, but if unchecked, that intensity can overwhelm others, leaving them feeling exhausted and that they do not measure up. The King of Wands must respect that people are allowed to lead their own lives, on their own terms.

When the King of Wands listens as well as speaks, supports as well as directs, they become not just a visionary but a deeply respected leader. For the King of Wands, needs to learn that strength lies not in domination but in the loyalty they inspire and the potential they release in others.

Relationships

The King of Wands brings intensity and deep-seated loyalty to their relationships. They love with the same fire that fuels their ambitions; passionately, protectively, and with a desire to uplift those they care about to ensure they fulfil their potential. Yet, this strength can sometimes make intimacy feel like a balancing act. They must learn that in a true partnership, one partner should not always take the dominant, leading role. Relationships are about listening, co-creating, compromising, and giving way. Though this may come unnaturally to the King of Wands, when they do this, when they accept and make space for their partner's emotional needs, the bond becomes unbreakable.

In love, they thrive with someone who shares their ideals and respects their strength but isn't afraid to walk beside them as an equal. When this happens, the partners can, together, become a powerful team, one that turns shared dreams into lived reality, driven by mutual respect and purpose.

Career and Purpose

The King of Wands is at their best when they are at the helm; commanding and leading. They thrive in positions of authority where their vision can be turned into strategy and action. Entrepreneurship, executive leadership, political advocacy, motivational speaking, or leading teams in high-stakes environments all suit their dynamic energy. They may also shine as a coach, in the military, or in the services, in any role where others look to them for bold direction and confident decision-making. In any career what defines their success is not only their own achievements, but the potential they awaken and bring to life in others. When their leadership uplifts and empowers, they fulfil their highest calling.

WHO AM I?

The court cards aren't just characters in a tarot deck; they're reflections of us. Each of us carries the essence of one of the sixteen personalities at our core, shaped by how we think, feel, and act in the world. The following two short quizzes are designed to help you discover which character and suit align most closely with your personality. While no label can fully define you, these results offer a starting point for self-understanding and deeper reflection. Are you a bold Knight or a compassionate King? Do you lead with emotion, thought, action, or stability?

Are you ready to find out?

There are two quizzes to complete. The first one helps you identify whether you most closely identify with the characters; Pages, Knights, Queens, or Kings, and the second quiz relates to the suits; Cups, Pentacles, Swords, and Wands. Read each question carefully and tick the option (or options) that feel most true to you. Don't overthink it, and go with your first instinct. If more than one answer resonates, it's fine to tick more than one. This quiz is about self-discovery, not about giving you a label, so be honest and curious with yourself.

Quizzes

Quiz 1

Which character am I?

1. When faced with something new I:
   a) Find out what the goal is and set a clear plan to follow.
   b) Reflect on how it aligns with my values before deciding whether to do it.
   c) Dive in enthusiastically and figure it out as I go along.
   d) Ask questions to understand what needs to be done and why.

2. I handle conflict by:
   a) Addressing it directly.
   b) Trying to find a compromise.
   c) Defending my position.
   d) Trying to avoid it.

3. I work best by:
   a) A structured approach.
   b) Collaborating with other people.
   c) Working things out as I come to them
   d) Understanding the reasons for doing it before I start

4. When making a big decision, I usually:
   a) Gather all the facts together and work out the pros and cons.
   b) Listen to my heart.
   c) Trust my instincts.
   d) Think long and hard about it before committing to one approach.

5. In a group situation I tend to:
   a) Take the lead.
   b) Observe.
   c) Keep things moving.
   d) Ask questions.

6. My idea of a successful life is:
   a) Building a legacy to leave something lasting for the next generation.
   b) Creating meaningful relationships.
   c) Having the personal freedom to do what I like.
   d) Continuously learning and experiencing new things.

7. I prefer to learn by:
   a) Structured lessons with clear outcomes.
   b) Working with others.
   c) Throwing myself into it.
   d) Exploring ideas, theories, and what-if scenarios.

8. When working with others I tend to:
   a) Take charge, organise and prioritise what needs to be done.
   b) Ensure everyone knows what they are doing and have what they need

c) Work on what I need to do, and let others sort themselves out.
d) Ensure I do what I need to do, but observe and learn from those around me

9. I most strongly associate with the following statement.
   a) "I am a natural leader and like to stay in control."
   b) "I'm a caregiver and often know how others feel before they speak."
   c) "I'm a doer, I just want to get things done"
   d) "I'm a seeker, always exploring, questioning, and learning."

10. Deadlines make me feel:
    a) Focused and productive.
    b) A little pressurised, but I know they are needed.
    c) Competitive, I see them as a challenge.
    d) Rushed, I feel I sometimes must compromise.

11. When helping others, I usually:
    a) Provide direction, and a clear way forward.
    b) Offer reassurance, and support.
    c) Step in and take action to fix things.
    d) Give guidance and help them consider their options.

12. I am most motivated by:
    a) Achievement
    b) Connections.
    c) Challenges.
    d) Personal growth.

How to Find Your Result:

Count how many of each letter (A, B, C, D) you selected:

- Mostly A's: You are a King – direct, capable, and built to lead.
- Mostly B's: You are a Queen – wise, nurturing, and emotionally intelligent.
- Mostly C's: You are a Knight – energetic, brave, and ready to take on the world.
- Mostly D's: You are a Page – curious, thoughtful, and eager to learn.

Quiz 2

To which suit do I belong?

1. When solving a problem, my first instinct is to:
    a. Work out how I feel about it.
    b. Look at it practically.
    c. Analyse it logically.
    d. Think of ways around it.

2. In a quiet moment, I would rather:
    a. Meditate, or spend time in quiet reflection.
    b. Go for a walk in nature.
    c. Read, or work on a puzzle.
    d. Tend to a hobby.

3. I approach life by:
    a. Following my heart.
    b. Going with the flow.
    c. Taking control.
    d. Chasing my dreams.

4. I am most fulfilled when:
   a. Helping others.
   b. Accomplishing something.
   c. Solving a problem.
   d. Starting something new

5. I get my energy from:
   a. Human connection.
   b. Nature
   c. Achieving something tangible
   d. Competition

6. My ideal holiday is:
   a. A villa by the sea.
   b. A cabin in the woods.
   a. A city break.
   b. An activity break.

7. When faced with change, I:
   a. Feel my way through it and seek emotional support.
   b. Prefer to ease in gradually and keep things stable.
   c. Try to understand it and make a strategy.
   d. Get excited and embrace the unknown.

8. I'm most motivated by
   a. Love and meaningful relationships.
   b. Security and achieving goals.
   c. Clarity of purpose and a plan.
   d. The freedom to go my own way.

9. If I was to choose one value above the others it would be:
   a. Kindness
   b. Reliability.
   c. Fairness.
   d. Creativity

10. I recharge my energy by:
    a. Meeting and talking with others.
    b. Rest and reflection.
    c. Working on a puzzle.
    d. Thinking up innovative ideas.

11. I react to pressure by:
    a. Talking it through with others.
    b. Staying calm and dealing with what's in front of me.
    c. Creating a plan.
    d. Throwing myself into whatever needs to be done.

12. My life's motto could be:
    a. "Feel it fully."
    b. "Build it steadily."
    c. "Understand it deeply."
    d. "Live it boldly."

Results: Count Your Answers

Count how many of each letter (A, B, C, D) you selected:

- Mostly A's: You are aligned with the Suit of Cups – emotional, empathetic, intuitive, and driven by connection and creativity.
- Mostly B's: You are aligned with the Suit of Pentacles – grounded, steady, practical, and focused on the physical and material world.
- Mostly C's: You are aligned with the Suit of Swords – analytical, wise, structured, and drawn to truth and mental clarity.
- Mostly D's: You are aligned with the Suit of Wands – energetic, passionate, future-focused, and bursting with inspiration.

About the Author

Andrew Laycock is a spiritual writer, teacher and coach. His books are available in paperback and ebook format.

Andrew lives in Dorset, on the south coast of the UK. He can often be found at mind, body, spirit events across the UK. He travels extensively and is happy to talk about his work at workshops and events.

To contact Andrew,

Email: andrew@wisdomguides.co.uk

Website: www.wisdomguides.co.uk

.

www.ingramcontent.com/pod-product-compliance
Lightning Source LLC
Chambersburg PA
CBHW051712040426
42446CB00008B/848